Extending the Hand of Fellowship

EXTENDING THE HAND OF FELLOWSHIP

The Relation of the Western Buddhist Order
to the Rest of the Buddhist World

SANGHARAKSHITA

WINDHORSE PUBLICATIONS

Published by Windhorse Publications
Unit 1-316 The Custard Factory,
Gibb Street
Birmingham, B9 4AA

Printed by Colbourne & Underwood
2 Lower Trinity Street
Birmingham, B9 4AG

Cover design Dhammarati

ISBN 0 904766 62 4

Preface

IN THIS, THE THIRD AND LAST PAPER in the series which began with 'The History of My Going for Refuge', Sangharakshita establishes the doctrinal basis upon which members of the Western Buddhist Order relate to the rest of the Buddhist world. And although that is the avowed intention of this paper, its significance goes much further. As Sangharakshita shows, Buddhism exists today in a very perilous state. In Tibet, China, Mongolia, Russia, Vietnam, Laos, and Cambodia it has been severely undermined by the forces of militant Communism. In Thailand, Taiwan, and Japan it is being undermined by consumerism, and in Sri Lanka and Myanmar, in different ways, it is undermined by militant nationalism. Only in India and the West does Buddhism seem to be in the ascendant.

We are living through an age of Buddhist decline on an unprecedented scale. But this is also an age of inter-Buddhist encounter. Never before have so many Buddhists been able to meet, face to face, with Buddhists of other sects, schools, and traditions; and never before has so much information about the different forms of Buddhism been so widely available.

This is a time, therefore, when Buddhists of all traditions most need to understand how to relate to each other. But despite this fact,

not until now has any Buddhist thinker concerned himself with the principles which underpin the relations between Buddhists of different traditions. This fact has significant practical implications: 'My relations with the Pope are better than with Zen or Theravada,' mused the Dalai Lama at a meeting with Western Buddhist teachers in 1993.

Ever since his first encounter with Buddhism at the age of sixteen, Sangharakshita has striven to understand Buddhism, not only in its heights and depths, but in its breadth as well. What other Theravadin Buddhist monk, in 1957, might have named his vihara, or monastery, the Triyana Vardana Vihara – the vihara where the Three Ways Flourish – in a gesture of ecumenism which explicitly recognized the intrinsic worth of the Northern, Southern, and Far Eastern Buddhist traditions?

As I travel around the Buddhist world on behalf of the FWBO's Liaison Office, I am struck again and again by the fact that, despite the enormous amount of goodwill which endures between Buddhists of different traditional allegiances, ignorance of the basic principles of inter-Buddhist dialogue leads, time and again, to breakdowns in communication.

'Welcome, Kulananda, how nice of you to come. We're just about to start lunch. Why don't you go over there and join in with the laity?'

My interlocutor was a smiling Theravadin Buddhist monk whom I'd come to visit at his monastery near London and, as Sangharakshita shows in this paper, I was being put in a false position. For although I am not a monk neither am I a layman. I am simply a committed Buddhist: one who effectively goes for Refuge to the Three Jewels.

So long as Buddhists relate to each other chiefly in terms of what is secondary – the number and type of precepts that they follow – or in terms of what is tertiary – their chosen life-style – rather than in terms of what is primary – the fact that we all, to whatever extent,

go for Refuge to the Three Jewels – then we will inevitably fail to communicate with each other.

In this paper, which was addressed to an audience of members of the Western Buddhist Order, Sangharakshita sets out the principles upon which genuine inter-Buddhist dialogue should be based. I believe that in our age of inter-Buddhist encounter and dialogue Sangharakshita's insights are relevant to all Buddhists everywhere. It is with just such a belief that this paper is now offered to a wider audience.

Dharmachari Kulananda
Madhyamaloka
April 1996

EXTENDING THE HAND OF FELLOWSHIP
The Relation of the Western Buddhist Order
to the Rest of the Buddhist World

IN APRIL 1988, AT A CELEBRATION marking the twentieth anniversary of the Western Buddhist Order, I read a paper in which I proposed to trace what I called the History of My Going for Refuge to the Three Jewels, as well as to share with my auditors some of my current thinking as regards my own relation to the Order and the relation of the Order itself to the rest of the Buddhist world. As it happened, the tracing of the various steps by which I had arrived at my understanding of the act of Going for Refuge as the central and definitive act of the Buddhist life took much longer than I had expected, and I was obliged to postpone my remarks on the two remaining subjects to some future occasion. Two years later, when the Order celebrated its twenty-second anniversary, I accordingly read a paper on My Relation to the Order. But this, too, became longer than I had expected, with the result that I was unable to say anything about the relation of the Order to the rest of the Buddhist world. Now, six years further on, when we are celebrating the twenty-eighth anniversary of the Order, I hope to be able to deal with the subject, thus bringing my original undertaking to a belated

conclusion. I shall take up the thread where I dropped it at the end of my paper on the History of My Going for Refuge. Having remarked that the nature of my relation to the Order had transpired to some extent in the latter part of the narrative, I continued:

> *As regards the relation of the Order to the rest of the Buddhist world let me simply observe that it is a relation that subsists, essentially, with individuals, and that, on this the occasion of our 20th anniversary, we are happy to extend the hand of spiritual fellowship to all those Buddhists for whom commitment is primary, lifestyle secondary, and who, like us, Go for Refuge to the Buddha, the Dharma, and the Sangha....*

The three principles here laid down, at least by implication, provide me with a point of departure for what I have to say today. Before embarking on the subject of our – the Order's – relation to the rest of the Buddhist world, however, I want to make a few remarks of a more general nature.

Since I spoke on the History of My Going for Refuge eight years have passed. Eight years is a long time, especially when one considers that it represents nearly one third of the time for which the Order has been in existence. During those eight years quite a lot has happened. In 1988 there were 336 Order members world-wide. Two years later there were 384. Today there are 654. With the growth of the Order – and it has grown not only numerically but in 'collective' experience and maturity – there has been a corresponding growth in its – and the FWBO's – activities. New public centres and residential spiritual communities, and even team-based right livelihood businesses, have sprung up, while old ones have expanded and diversified. Books have been written, new magazines launched, and films produced. One might be forgiven for thinking that there was no end to what had happened, both externally and, what is no less important, in terms of the achievement, by individual Order members, of a deeper experience of Going for Refuge by means of

ethical living, meditation, Dharma study, spiritual friendship, community life, and ritual and devotion. For me personally the most important thing to have happened in the course of the last eight years is that I have been able to hand on many of my responsibilities as founder and head of the Order to a team of some dozen Order members, especially those comprising the College of Public Preceptors. Soon, I hope, *all* those responsibilities will have been handed on – at least to the extent that this is possible while I am still physically present among you. As you know, last year I celebrated my seventieth birthday, or rather you (and the rest of the Movement) celebrated it and I simply enjoyed the celebrations, and I feel it to be incumbent upon me, during such time as I have left, to do whatever I can to ensure the continuity, well-being, and growth of the Movement after my departure from the scene. This includes sharing with you my current thinking about the Dharma in general and our own tradition in particular, and this is one of the reasons I am addressing you today on the Relation of the Order to the Rest of the Buddhist World.

I have, of course, been anticipated by Subhuti, who in 1991 gave a talk on 'Relations with Other Buddhists'. In this talk he explored the subject under the three principal headings of the Need for Clarity, History of the FWBO's Relations with Other Groups, and Principles behind our Contact with Others, each of which enabled him to touch on a variety of issues and make a number of important points. This paper will be much more limited in scope, as I shall be dealing with the relation of the Order, specifically, to the rest of the Buddhist world, as well as having more to say about that world itself. Subhuti's talk and my paper may therefore be regarded as complementary, and best read in conjunction with each other, even though there is a small amount of overlap between them. In any case, Subhuti has his style, and I have mine. Perhaps it is also relevant to observe that during the last four or five years I have had more personal contact with leading Western Buddhists, both

European and North American, than I had in the course of the preceding twenty years.

But it is time I returned to the three principles that were laid down, at least by implication, in the remarks with which I concluded my paper on the History of My Going for Refuge and which provide me with a point of departure now. These three principles may be designated, for convenience, the principle of ecumenicity, as represented by the words 'the relation of the Order to the rest of the Buddhist world,' the principle of personal contact, as represented by the words 'it is a relation that subsists, essentially, with individuals,' and the principle of orthodoxy, as represented by the words 'we are happy to extend the hand of spiritual fellowship to all those Buddhists for whom commitment is primary, lifestyle secondary, and who, like us, Go for Refuge to the Buddha, the Dharma, and the Sangha.' For the sake of connectedness of exposition I shall be dealing with the second and third principles in reverse order.

The Principle of Ecumenicity

It may not have escaped your notice that I spoke, in my paper on the History of My Going for Refuge, not of the relation of the Order to the Buddhist world but of the relation of the Order to the *rest* of the Buddhist world. The word was intended to emphasize the fact that the Order, and with it the FWBO, is a branch of the mighty tree of Buddhism which, for more than 2,500 years, has sheltered a considerable portion of humanity, and that the same vital juice that circulates in the older, bigger branches of that tree circulates in our younger, smaller branch too, even if it circulates in it a little more vigorously than it does in some of them. It is important that we should not only acknowledge this intellectually but also feel it. After all, our doctrinal teachings and methods of meditation, together with our terminology and our iconography, derive

exclusively from traditional Buddhist sources, and we therefore might be expected to experience a sense of solidarity with the spiritual and cultural œcumene of which we form a part and with which, moreover, we might be expected to want to be in communication.

But what is this Buddhist world? Most certainly it is not a central-ized world like that of Roman Catholicism, with its Pope and its Vatican, and its sacramental and catechetical uniformity. Notwith-standing the establishment of the World Fellowship of Buddhists in 1950, so few and so tenuous are the threads connecting the different parts of the Buddhist world that *effectively* no such thing as a Buddhist world really exists. Instead we have a number of sectarian Buddhist worlds which are divided one from another along doctrinal and other lines and which have – to revert to my previous metaphor – in some cases diverged so widely from the parent trunk that they have difficulty seeing themselves as branches of the same tree or feeling that an identical sap circulates through every one of them. According to the older Western writers on Buddhism there were two such worlds, that of Northern Buddh-ism and that of Southern Buddhism. In reality, however, the former consisted of two separate worlds, that of Northern Buddhism proper and that of Far Eastern Buddhism. Thus we may speak of there being, in the broadest sense, three Buddhist worlds, though these are such not only geographically and culturally but doctri-nally and spiritually as well. Southern Buddhism is synonymous with the Theravada, the School or Teaching of the Elders, which is found principally in Sri Lanka, Myanmar (Burma), Thailand, Cam-bodia, and Laos. Northern Buddhism corresponds to the Triyana Buddhism of Tibet (I am ignoring present-day political realities), Mongolia, and Bhutan, together with parts of Nepal, India, and Russia, wherein elements of the Hinayana and the Mahayana are subsumed in a synthesis the overall orientation of which is that of the Vajrayana or Tantric Buddhism. Far Eastern Buddhism is that

form of the Buddhist religion which predominates in (Han) China, Japan, Korea, and Vietnam. Here elements of the Hinayana and, though to a much more limited extent, of the Vajrayana, are subsumed in a synthesis the overall emphasis of which is that of the Mahayana. All three forms of Buddhism, it should be noted, subsume substantial elements of local, indigenous ethnic culture, some of which are not always content to remain within the bounds prescribed for them.

It is also possible to speak of five Buddhist worlds and five forms of Buddhism, with one of the forms, the Theravada, belonging to the Hinayana, and the remaining four to the Mahayana. This is what I have done, in effect, in *A Survey of Buddhism*, where having described the different characteristics of the Hinayana and the Mahayana in Chapter II, in Chapter III I utilize the teaching of the five (spiritual) faculties or indriyas as a principle for the schematization of the Mahayana schools. Applying this principle, I was able to arrive at a list of four movements within the Mahayana, which eventually crystallized into four schools. There was an intellectual movement that represented a development of the faculty of wisdom (*prajñā*) and found expression in the Madhyamikavada or New Wisdom School[1], a devotional movement that represented a development of the faculty of faith (*śraddhā*) and found expression in the Buddhism of Faith and Devotion, a meditative movement that represented a development of the faculty of meditation (*samādhi*) and found expression in the Yogachara-Vijnanavada or Buddhist Idealism, and an activistic movement that represented the faculty of vigour (*vīrya*) and found expression in the Tantra, or Magical Buddhism. Mindfulness (*smṛti*), the fifth (spiritual) faculty, was represented in the history of Buddhism by the various syncretist movements which from time to time endeavoured to bring the different schools into harmony. Out of the four Mahayana schools here enumerated, three have not only survived in the East as distinct forms of Buddhism down to the present but also have been

introduced in the West. Thus the Buddhism of Faith and Devotion appears in our midst as Pure Land Buddhism, Buddhist Idealism as Zen, and the Tantra as Tibetan Buddhism. The teachings of the New Wisdom School survive as an important element in both Zen and Tibetan Buddhism. As for the Theravada, this has of course survived in the East as a distinct form of Buddhism down to the present and appears in our midst in various South-east Asian garbs.

In speaking of the relation of the Order to the rest of the Buddhist world one is therefore speaking of it as having, for all practical purposes, four separate relations, one to the Theravada, one to Pure Land Buddhism, one to Zen, and one to Tibetan Buddhism, each of which inhabits a world of its own, with its distinctive manners and customs, even its distinctive atmosphere, and which more often than not is only vaguely aware of the greater Buddhist world to which, in principle, it belongs. In each case the nature of the relation will be determined, at least to an extent, by certain developments within the form of Buddhism to which the Order happens to be relating, as will transpire in the next section of this paper, when I deal with the principle of orthodoxy. Let me therefore conclude this section by saying something about the more general characteristics of the Theravada, of Pure Land Buddhism, of Zen, and of Tibetan Buddhism, especially in so far as these characteristics constitute for us in the Order, as well as throughout the FWBO, a source of inspiration and spiritual guidance. First, however, I want to say a few words about the Buddhist world in the geographical sense.

In the course of my lifetime, at least, the portion of the earth's surface traditionally covered by Buddhism has shrunk dramatically. This fact is highlighted, with stark clarity, in an article published in a recent issue of *Tricycle*. Commenting on the undermining of Buddhism in Tibet, China, Mongolia, Vietnam, Laos, and Cambodia through the destruction of the monastic framework upon which the Buddhist community in those countries depended, Stephen Batchelor writes:

Indeed, it is remarkable to compare the extent of the Buddhist world fifty years ago with what remains today. Never in human history has such a major world religion diminished in size and influence so rapidly. Three or four revolutions in the right places would more or less eliminate traditional Buddhism from the face of the earth.[2]

It is a sobering thought, especially when we consider that during the last fifty years both Christianity and Islam have expanded enormously (though not at the expense of Buddhism itself), with the result that Buddhism is now the smallest and in certain respects the least influential of the three great world religions. The only bright spots in an otherwise quite gloomy picture are India, where up to ten million followers of the late Dr B.R. Ambedkar have become Buddhists in recent years, and Western Europe, the Americas, and Australasia, where the seed of the Buddha's teaching is steadily taking root in the hearts of thousands of practitioners. Even in those Buddhist countries which have not suffered under Communism, like Thailand and Japan, the demands of consumerism are eroding traditional values and the way of life based on them. Those values are also being eroded by the behaviour of some of their official custodians. On the very day I started writing this paper came the news that a Thai monk addicted to amphetamines had been charged with murdering and robbing a 23-year-old English woman solicitor missing for more than a month on a backpacking holiday. The monk confessed that three days before committing the murder he had raped another woman tourist. Giving details of the case, the South-east Asia correspondent of a leading daily wrote:

Buddhism in Thailand has been rocked by a series of scandals in recent months. A revered abbot was charged with raping hill tribe girls in his care, a preacher was unfrocked amid allegations of sexual impropriety; a novice was arrested for roasting a still-born baby on a spit in a black magic ritual and six monks were charged with murdering a fellow monk.[3]

Scandals have also rocked the Tibetan diaspora in India, where there were unseemly dissensions between the supporters of rival candidates for the throne of the deceased Karmapa, the immensely wealthy head of the Karma Kagyu School. In the course of these dissensions acts of violence were committed, and an eminent lama died in what many regarded as suspicious circumstances.[4] While we must be careful not to extrapolate too freely from the facts, occurrences such as those reported from Thailand and the Tibetan diaspora suggest that, undermined as it is both from without and within, traditional Buddhism is in a state of decline, and that committed Buddhists everywhere need to give serious thought to the question of how best to preserve the Dharma for the benefit of future generations. One of the ways in which we of the Western Buddhist Order can help preserve the Dharma is by acquainting ourselves with the general characteristics of the Theravada, of Pure Land Buddhism, of Zen, and of Tibetan Buddhism, especially in so far as these characteristics constitute a source of inspiration and spiritual guidance to us, and it is to the four schools and their scriptures that we must now turn.

The Theravada is based on the Pali Tipitaka or 'Three Baskets', that is to say, the Vinaya-Pitaka, the basket or collection of monastic discipline, the Sutta-Pitaka, the basket or collection of the Buddha's sayings and discourses, and the Abhidhamma-Pitaka, the basket or collection of further, i.e. more 'philosophical', teaching, as well as upon the various commentaries to these texts. So far, at least, we have tended to derive inspiration and guidance from what appear to be the older portions of the Tipitaka, especially from the *Sutta-nipata*, the *Udana*, the *Itivuttaka*, the *Dhammapada*, and the *Thera*- and *Theri-gatha*, all of which belong to the Sutta-Pitaka, as do the *Digha*- and *Majjhima-Nikayas*, select discourses from which are also a source of inspiration and guidance for some of us. The only non-canonical Theravadin text to which we have regular recourse is Buddhaghosa's *Visuddhi-magga*, the second section of which, on

samadhi, is particularly useful. All the texts I have mentioned inculcate harmlessness, non-attachment, tranquillity, contentment, forbearance, kindness, mindfulness, effort, and discrimination, and it is these which are the general characteristics of the Theravada, at its best, as well as being among the essential, definitive qualities of the spiritual life. The same texts also give us, between them, a more vivid impression of the Buddha in his (enlightened) human, historical reality than do any other scriptures, with the possible exception of such portions of the Sanskrit counterpart of the Sutta-Pitaka as survive in the original language or in Chinese or Tibetan translation. This does not mean that the historical necessarily excludes the 'legendary'. As Reginald A. Ray has lately reminded us:

> *Western and modernist notions of a demythologized individuality standing apart from and independent of symbol, cult, and legend have no relevance for the early Buddhist case. Gautama, in his own time and in subsequent times, was able to be the Buddha precisely because he was understood to embody, in an unprecedented way, the cosmic and transcendent. Far from being incidental to who he was, myth and cult define his essential person, for his earliest followers as for later Buddhists.*[5]

In my own words, commenting on Ray's assertion, 'we come closest to the historical Buddha precisely when we take the legendary and cultic idiom of his hagiographical tradition most seriously.'[6] That we are able to come close to the Buddha at all, and to derive inspiration and guidance from his personal example as well as from his actual teaching, is largely owing to the fact that we have access to the older portions of the Tipitaka, and we are accordingly grateful to the Theravada for having preserved them. Various selections from the Pali canon illustrative of the Buddha's life as well as of his teaching are available. One of the best of these is Bhikkhu Nanamoli's *The Life of the Buddha*, which is well known to many of us, as is Dr B.R. Ambedkar's *The Buddha and His Dhamma*.

The three remaining schools, being schools of the Mahayana, are all based, ultimately, on the Mahayana sutras, though they may have a closer connection with some sutras than with others. There are hundreds of Mahayana sutras, by no means all of which have been translated into any European language. Those from which we have so far derived the greatest inspiration and guidance – and they happen to be among the most important Mahayana scriptures – are the *Prajna-paramita* Sutras, especially the Diamond and Heart Sutras, the *Saddharma-pundarika Sutra*, the *Vimalakirti-nirdesa*, and the *Suvarna-prabhasa Sutra*. All these works are distinguished by universality of outlook, philosophical profundity, and a willingness, on the part of most of them, to communicate spiritual truths by non-conceptual means – all of which are general characteristics of the schools based on them. They all proclaim, moreover, the Bodhisattva ideal, the ideal of absolute spiritual altruism, which in one form or other is the chosen ideal of all schools of the Mahayana.

Pure Land Buddhism is based on the two *Sukhavati-vyuha* Sutras, the Larger and the Smaller, and on the *Amitayur-dhyana Sutra*. All three works describe Sukhavati, 'the Blissful', the pure land of the Buddha Amitabha, as well as describing Amitabha (or Amitayus) himself and his two Bodhisattva attendants. A pure land, as distinct from one that is impure, is an archetypal realm which transcends conditioned existence and which apart from the presiding Buddha and his Bodhisattvas is inhabited exclusively by gods and men. There are hundreds of thousands of such pure lands, but the most excellent of them is Sukhavati, the pure land of Buddha Amitabha, in which are concentrated all imaginable perfections of all imaginable pure lands. In other words what we are presented with, in these three sutras, is the vision of an ideally beautiful Buddha in ideally beautiful surroundings. The contemplation of beauty gives rise to love, and when the beauty contemplated is the sublime beauty of Buddhahood, as manifested in the radiant figure of Amitabha, that love takes the form of faith and devotion, through

which the devotee is assimilated to the object of his devotion and achieves, in the symbolic language of the sutras, rebirth in Sukhavati. As yet, the Order as a whole has not paid much attention to the three Happy Land sutras (as I have called them elsewhere), and therefore has not derived much inspiration and guidance from them, though I myself made a close study of them many years ago and at one time thought of lecturing on them, as I had done on other Mahayana sutras. But though we may not derive inspiration and guidance from this group of sutras directly, in a way we do so indirectly. Many Buddhas besides Amitabha, as well as many Bodhisattvas, have pure lands of their own, some of which are described in sutras. Like the Happy Land sutras, these texts establish a kind of pattern, in which a figure embodying the ideal of Enlightenment occupies the centre of a realm representing the conditions most conducive to the realization of that ideal. This pattern is exemplified in many of our sadhanas, in the course of which we visualize at the centre of a mandala of other divinities, or of the syllables of a mantra, a Buddha or Bodhisattva who is the object of our faith and devotion and, at the same time, a source of inspiration and guidance. Some of us also derive inspiration from the various hymns in praise of this or that Bodhisattva which, though they may not be a part of Pure Land Buddhism in the Japanese sectarian form in which we usually encounter this school in the West, are none the less a product of that Buddhism of Faith and Devotion of which Pure Land Buddhism, in all its forms, is itself a part.

Zen claims not to be based on any sutra or group of sutras. In the words of the well-known stanza in which it summarizes itself and defines its attitude, it is a special transmission *outside the scriptures*, does not depend upon words and letters, points directly to the mind, and points to the realization of Buddhahood by seeing into one's own nature. Historically speaking, however, Zen seems to have come into existence, in its original form as Ch'an, among a

group of Chinese students of the *Lankavatara Sutra*, though later the work was superseded by the *Diamond Sutra* and, to a lesser extent, by the *Surangama Sutra* and the *Vimalakirti-nirdesa*. For practical purposes, Zen bases itself on collections of anecdotes of the sayings and doings of ancient masters of the school such as the *Blue Cliff Record* and the *Gateless Gate*. Despite its aversion to scriptural studies it has in fact produced a vast literature, little of which has been translated into any European language. Probably the classic Zen texts from which we in the Order have derived most inspiration are the *Sutra of Wei Lang* (Hui Neng), otherwise known as the *Platform Scripture*, and Hakuin's 'Song of Enlightenment', both of which are characterized by an emphasis on the necessity of direct realization of the highest spiritual truth. For some of us inspiration also comes from Zen by way of the poetry of Bashō and Ryōkan, with its appreciation of natural beauty, its sympathy for all forms of life, and its total disregard of unessentials, as well as by way of those other 'arts' which, under the influence of Zen, were transformed into paths to Enlightenment. Nor must I forget to mention the words of the T'ang dynasty master Pai-chang which, after reverberating down the centuries and creating a distinctively Zen form of monasticism, have influenced our ideas about how the Movement and its activities should be supported – the famous words, 'A day of no working is a day of no eating.'

Tibetan Buddhism is based on the Kangyur and Tangyur and, in the case of some of its subdivisions, on the *Rinchen Termo*, as well as on a variety of orally transmitted teachings. Broadly speaking, it represents a transplantation to the soil of Tibet of the entire heritage of Buddhist spirituality, thought, and culture as this existed in Northern India at the time of the Pala dynasty. Prominent among the works of Tibetan origin from which we in the Order have so far derived inspiration and guidance are the *Bardo-thodol*, better known as the *Tibetan Book of the Dead*, the biography and songs of Milarepa, the *Life and Liberation of Padmasambhava*, Gampopa's *Jewel Ornament*

of Liberation, and the various texts translated in Geshe Wangyal's *Door of Liberation*. It is noteworthy that two of these works, the *Tibetan Book of the Dead* and the *Life and Liberation of Padmasambhava*, are Nyingma termas, while the biography and songs of Milarepa and Gampopa's *Jewel Ornament of Liberation* are of Kagyu provenance. Both the *Tibetan Book of the Dead* and the *Life and Liberation of Padmasambhava*, moreover, are characterized by extreme richness of imagery – a richness that characterizes Tibetan Buddhism as a whole, especially in its ritual and iconographic aspects. Probably it is in the archetypal images of Tibetan religious art, even more than in their literary counterparts in the two termas, that many of us find a great part of the inspiration we derive from Tibetan Buddhism. Be that as it may, there is no doubt that Tibetan Buddhist iconography is popular throughout the Euro-American wing of the Movement, though for my part I would like to see Japanese Buddhist art enjoying equal popularity.

Such, then, are the general characteristics of the Theravada, of Pure Land Buddhism, of Zen, and of Tibetan Buddhism, especially in so far as these characteristics constitute for us in the Order, as well as throughout the FWBO, a source of inspiration and spiritual guidance. We derive that inspiration and guidance, however, not so much from these schools in the form in which they survive in the East, and have been introduced in the West, as from a selection of the scriptures on which, in principle, they respectively are based. As I pointed out when speaking of the Buddhist world, traditional Buddhism, undermined as it is both without and within, is in a state of decline. Actually it has been in a state of decline for a very long time, in that all four schools, in their different ways and in varying degrees, have tended to emphasize what is secondary in Buddhism at the expense of what is primary. This fact has an important bearing on the whole question of the relation of the Order to the rest of the Buddhist world, or rather, to the schools of which, for

practical purposes, it consists so far as we are concerned. Which brings me to the second of my three principles.

The Principle of Orthodoxy

In 1957 I wrote an essay entitled 'The Meaning of Orthodoxy in Buddhism'. I wrote it in response to the assertion, by a leading Pali scholar, that the Theravada 'was certainly the most orthodox form of Buddhism',[7] a description which effectively asserted, with equal decision, that the non-Theravadin schools were less orthodox, or unorthodox, or even positively heretical. In this essay, having pointed out that the exact literal equivalent of 'orthodoxy' (from the Greek *ortho*, right, true + *doxos*, opinion) was right view, I defined orthodoxy, in the Buddhist sense, as '1. Of Right Views (*sammādiṭṭhika*); hence, adhering to the Dharma of the Buddha as formulated in the stereotype formulae such as the Four Noble Truths and the Three Characteristics (*tilakkhana*) without inclining either to the extreme of Eternalism (*sassatavada*) or the extreme of Nihilism (*ucchedavāda*); – opposed to Wrong Views (*micchādiṭṭhi*), both in the wider sense of the erroneous beliefs of non-Buddhists and the narrower one of a misunderstanding of the Dharma by one who has taken the Three Refuges; as, an *orthodox* bhikshu. 2. According to, or congruous with, the doctrines of the Scriptures common to all schools of Buddhism, especially as expressed in the stereotype formulae such as the Four Noble Truths and the Three Characteristics (*tri-lakṣaṇa*) which are found in both the Scriptures which are and the Scriptures which are not common to all schools; as, an *orthodox* opinion, book, etc. 3. Conventional, a matter not of natural (*pakati*) but of conventional (*paññati*) Morality; as, an *orthodox* prostration.'[8] This definition enabled me to vindicate the doctrinal and scriptural orthodoxy of the Mahayana and to show that the orthodoxy of the Theravada was not a matter of so much certainty as had been supposed. It also enabled me to distinguish

between an orthodox Buddhist and an orthodox Mahayana or Hinayana Buddhist and, by implication, between an orthodox Buddhist and an unorthodox Buddhist.

But what is an orthodox Buddhist? At the time of writing 'The Meaning of Orthodoxy in Buddhism' I did not realize the absolute centrality, in the genuinely Buddhist life, of the act of Going for Refuge, or rather, though I realized it to some extent I had not yet worked out its implications. I therefore did not connect the principle of orthodoxy with the fact of the absolute centrality of the act of Going for Refuge. Now, thirty-nine years later, the time has come for that connection to be made. To put it briefly, and in terms with which we are familiar, an orthodox Buddhist is one for whom Going for Refuge is primary, observance of the precepts secondary, or better still, one for whom Going for Refuge is primary, observance of the precepts (and practice of meditation etc.) secondary, and life-style tertiary. From this it follows that one for whom the act of Going for Refuge is not the central, definitive act of the Buddhist life is *not* an orthodox Buddhist, even though they may have formally 'taken' the Three Refuges and be professed adherents of orthodox Buddhism as defined in my essay. Indeed, going a step further and taking a plunge into paradox, it could even be asserted that there is in truth no such thing as orthodox Buddhism but only orthodox Buddhists, that is, Buddhists for whom Going for Refuge is primary, observance of the precepts secondary, and lifestyle tertiary. But paradox or no paradox, we have to take into account the fact that the followers of the four schools in connection with which, for all practical purposes, the question of the relation between the Order and the rest of the Buddhist world arises, are not, *in this sense*, orthodox Buddhists. They are not orthodox Buddhists because, for them, something other than Going for Refuge is of primary importance in the Buddhist life, at least in practice, and the fact that such is the case affects the nature of our relation to them as, indeed, it affects the nature of their relation to us.

At the beginning of this paper, quoting from the end of my paper on the History of My Going for Refuge, I spoke of our being happy to extend the hand of spiritual fellowship 'to all those Buddhists for whom commitment is primary, lifestyle secondary, and who, like us, Go for Refuge to the Buddha, the Dharma, and the Sangha.' This might be taken to mean that we are happy to extend the hand of spiritual fellowship only to *orthodox* Buddhists. It was not my intention to impose any such limitation. There are degrees of spiritual fellowship, as we shall see when we come to the third of my three principles, the principle of personal contact. Meanwhile, we have to get to grips with the principle with which we are at present concerned, the principle of orthodoxy, and examine the different ways in which the Theravada, Pure Land Buddhism, Zen, and Tibetan Buddhism, emphasize what is secondary in the Buddhist life at the expense of what is primary, or in other words, the different ways in which they are unorthodox rather than orthodox.

The Theravada places its emphasis fairly and squarely on monasticism, on being a monk (*bhikkhu*) not a layman. It is the yellow-robed monk who is the real Buddhist, the white-clad layman or laywoman (and even the 'nun', whether Sinhalese dasasilamata or Thai maeje) being at best only a second-class Buddhist whose principal duty is to support the monk. Thus the Theravada's emphasis is on lifestyle, despite the fact that the traditional Refuge-Going formula is well known to all Theravadin Buddhists and is ceremonially recited, in Pali, by monks and laity alike. Nor is that all. In actual practice, more often than not, it is not so much the spirit as the letter of monasticism which is emphasized, great importance being attached, in particular, to valid monastic ordination in the technical Vinaya sense, with the result that although some of the general characteristics of the true Theravada certainly do shine through, here and there, today the school as a whole is vitiated by that very formalism of which the Buddha himself, according to the older portions of the Theravada's own Pali

Tipitaka, was so persistently critical. I have given examples of this formalism in *A Survey of Buddhism* and, more recently, in *Was the Buddha a Bhikkhu?*, and there is no need for me to enlarge upon the subject in this paper. Here I am concerned not so much with the Theravada's emphasis on monasticism as with the way in which that emphasis affects our relation to this school and this school's relation to us. But before I turn to the relation of the Order to the Theravada let me make a general point in connection with this question of formalism. Though I have tended, in my writings, to criticize only Theravadin formalism, it should not be thought that other forms of Buddhism are free from this canker. The reason for my criticizing Theravadin formalism, specifically, was that it was Theravadin formalism which, in my early days in India, I came across, not to say came up against. Subsequently I became aware that formalism, whether monastic or non-monastic, was a feature of much traditional Buddhism, almost regardless of school. It was, indeed, a danger that threatened the integrity of the religious life in all its forms and one against which even orthodox Buddhists needed to be on their guard.

As the Theravada places its emphasis on monasticism, even on monasticism in the merely formal sense, it sees the Buddhist community as being divided into two distinct groups. On the one hand there are the monks, who are the real Buddhists, on the other there are the laity (including the 'nuns'), who are the not-so-real Buddhists, as I once called them, who are expected to feed, clothe, and generally support the monks, and to observe in their dealings with them a protocol expressive of the profoundest veneration. But to which of these groups do members of the Western Buddhist Order/Trailokya Bauddha Mahasangha belong? So far as the Theravada is concerned the answer is obvious. They belong to the second group, that of the laity, for not having received bhikkhu ordination (there is no question of bhikkhuni ordination, in the case of women Order members) they are not monks, and there is no

other group to which those who are *not* monks *could* belong. Hence when a Theravadin monk meets an Order member – and it is usually a Theravadin monk, not a Theravadin layman, especially on 'official' occasions – he will automatically assume that, as the latter obviously is not a monk, he is a layman. As a layman he will therefore treat him, expecting that the Order member, in his turn, will treat *him* as a monk, with all that this implies. In these circumstances it is not surprising that there should sometimes arise situations which would be comical were they not based on a lamentable misunderstanding, on the part of the Theravadin monk, of a fundamental principle of the Dharma, the principle, namely, that spiritual attainment has little or nothing to do with socio-religious status, and that one is no more a bhikkhu, in the true sense, simply because one has been 'ordained' and wears a yellow robe, than one is a real brahmin simply because one has been born into a 'brahmin' family and wears a sacred thread. An Order member might even find himself (or herself) in the position of being condescendingly 'put right' as regards Buddhism by a globe-trotting career monk who obviously had no feeling for the spiritual life. On the other hand, it is important that when an Order member meets a Theravadin monk he (or she) should be open to the possibility that the monk is a real monk, even an orthodox Buddhist, and that it might be possible for one to relate to him not as though one was a 'layman', which would mean not really relating to him at all, but on the basis of one's being an Order member, that is, on the basis of one's Going for Refuge, effectively at least, to the Buddha, the Dharma, and the Sangha. Although there are incomparably more Theravadin monks in the East than there are in the West, an Order member probably stands a better chance of meeting a real monk, *and* of being able to relate to him on the basis of a common commitment to the Three Jewels, in the West than in the Theravadin lands of South-east Asia. In the latter the Theravada is still firmly based on what Reginald A. Ray calls the two-tiered model of Buddhism, which makes it difficult

for Buddhists who do not accept that model to extend the hand of spiritual fellowship either literally or metaphorically. How the difficulty might best be overcome we shall see in connection with the principle of personal contact.

Although the Theravada places its emphasis on monasticism, in recent decades there has arisen within its fold a predominantly lay movement, generally known as the vipassana or 'insight meditation' movement, which emphasizes what is secondary in Buddhism at the expense of what is primary in a different way. This movement, now well represented in the West, had its origins in Myanmar (Burma), in the efforts of a handful of monk and lay teachers to revive and popularize the practice of mindful awareness as taught by the Buddha in his discourse on the Foundations of Mindfulness. Nowadays, unfortunately, some of the movement's leading personalities not only emphasize meditation, in the sense of 'insight meditation', at the expense of Going for Refuge; they also ignore Going for Refuge completely. In extreme cases, having reduced meditation to 'vipassana', and vipassana itself to a matter of mere technique, they take it out of its Buddhist context and seek to combine it with elements derived from other sources, so that it is no longer vipassana in the traditional sense but something quite different. To the extent that one is a practitioner of this non-Buddhist 'vipassana' one is not a Buddhist, whether of the Theravada or any other school, and there can be no question of an Order member relating to such a person on the basis of a common Going for Refuge, though he (or she) may relate to them positively in other ways.

The fact that the Order does not emphasize monasticism does not mean that there is no place for it within our ranks. There is certainly a place for Sutra-style monasticism, as I have called it in *Forty-Three Years Ago*, though there is a place for it only as an *expression* of commitment to the Three Jewels, not as *constitutive* of that commitment, and I am glad to see that since I wrote that little book, three

years ago, the number of Order members observing the training rule of chastity as anagarikas has doubled, from twenty-odd to forty-odd. Similarly, the fact that the Order does not emphasize meditation, in the sense of 'insight meditation', at the expense of Going for Refuge, does not mean that there is no place in it for vipassana in the more traditional form which is common, in principle, to practically all schools of Buddhism. Much less still does it mean that we do not regard the development of both calm (*śamathā*) and insight (*vipaśyanā*) as essential elements in our spiritual life.

If the Theravada places its emphasis on monasticism, then the Jōdo Shinshū – the form of Pure Land Buddhism we are most likely to encounter in the West – goes to the opposite extreme and places it, in practice, on the laical life. This is not to say that it emphasizes the laical life in principle. In principle it places its emphasis on birth in Sukhavati through faith in the compassion of the Buddha Amitabha, especially as this finds expression in his famous Eighteenth Vow, according to which he would not gain Buddhahood unless those who had faith in him, and who wished to be born in his Pure Land, should be born there when he had gained it. Since he has, in fact, gained Buddhahood, it follows that those who have faith in him are assured of such birth. Nevertheless the Jōdo Shinshū also distinguishes between the path of dependence on 'self power' (*jiriki*), which is the path followed by other schools, and the path of dependence on 'other power' (*tariki*), that is, on the power of Amitabha's vow, which is the path the Jōdo Shinshū itself follows. Monasticism, with its numerous rules, obviously belongs to the path of dependence on 'self power', and as such it has no place in the form of Pure Land Buddhism represented by the Jōdo Shinshū. Since there was no question of their being monks, followers of the school were lay people by default, as it were, for although Shinran Shōnin, the school's 13th century founder, described himself as being neither a monk nor a layman, he married and raised a family and was in effect a layman. Rennyo, the eighth head priest

in succession to Shinran, who is honoured as the second founder of the Jōdo Shinshū, married seven times and had twenty-seven children, his youngest son being born when he was in his 85th year. Thus there is in practice a definite emphasis on the laical life in the Jōdo Shinshū, even though there would appear to be nothing in the school's teaching to prevent its followers from living as monks (or nuns) out of gratitude to Amitabha for having assured them of birth in Sukhavati. In the Order we of course follow the path of dependence on 'self power', as the very fact of our going for Refuge to the Three Jewels and undertaking to observe the Ten Precepts indeed implies. This does not however mean that what may be experienced, in relation to the ego, as an 'other power', may not come into operation at a certain stage of our spiritual development.

It is well known that 'zen' is the Japanese form of the Chinese word 'ch'an', which is itself a corruption of the Sanskrit 'dhyana', usually rendered in English as 'meditation'. Thus the Zen school is the meditation school. Whether in the form of zazen or 'just sitting' practice favoured by its Sōtō branch, or in that of the koan practice favoured by its Rinzai branch, the emphasis of the Zen school falls unambiguously on meditation. According to tradition the Buddha gained Enlightenment while meditating beneath a peepul tree. Meditation is one of the three practices which he is represented, in the Pali scriptures, as time and again recommending to his disciples during the last months of his life, the two other practices being right conduct (*sīla*) and wisdom (*paññā*). Small wonder, then, that the Zen school should emphasize meditation. Unfortunately, it came to emphasize it at the expense of Going for Refuge, besides falling victim to formalism in the practice of meditation itself. Abbot Tenshin Anderson, a leading North American teacher of Zen, confesses:

For many years at Zen Center I had never really noticed that I had taken refuge in Buddha, Dharma, Sangha.... This basic practice, this

fundamental practice, which all Buddhists do, many Zen students never even heard about. It was said, but we didn't hear it, because it wasn't emphasized strongly enough. In some way our sitting practice is so essential, so profound, that we feel that we can overlook some of the more basic practices.[9]

That anyone should *not notice* that they had 'taken refuge' in the Three Jewels seems incredible, and the failure may well be connected with the fact that Abbot Anderson, like so many Western Buddhists, speaks of a *taking* rather than of a *going*. Be that as it may, a sitting practice so profound that one can 'overlook' something as basic as Going for Refuge is hardly profound in the Buddhist sense, particularly when basic means, in this context, not elementary but fundamental to the living of the Buddhist life in all its aspects and at every level. Moreover, the lack of emphasis on 'taking refuge' of which Tenshin Anderson speaks makes it all the more easy for 'Zen' to be detached from Buddhism and even taught by non-Buddhists, in which case it is no more truly Zen than non-Buddhist 'vipassana' is vipassana in the traditional sense. Another leading North American teacher, Roshi Philip Kapleau, does not hesitate to cite 'the appropriation of fundamental elements of Zen training by psychotherapists teaching their patients meditation and equating it with spiritual liberation' as an example of the *real* corruption in Buddhism, nor to speak of 'Zen teachers sanctioning Catholic priests and nuns as well as rabbis and ministers to teach Zen' as being in many ways the most bizarre of all the threats to the integrity of Zen.[10]

Tibetan Buddhism is probably a richer and more complex phenomenon than any of the other schools with which, for all practical purposes, the Order's relation to the rest of the Buddhist world consists. In fact it comprises not one school but many, each with its own teachings, practices, and institutions. These schools all operate, however, within the framework of a common theoretical and practical schema, that of the three yanas, the three 'vehicles' or

'ways', i.e. the Hinayana, the Mahayana, and the Vajrayana, to one or other of which all the different doctrines and methods of Tibetan Buddhism are systematically assigned. Thus Going for Refuge is assigned to the Hinayana, the arising of the Bodhichitta or Will to Enlightenment to the Mahayana, and abhishekha or 'Tantric initiation' to the Vajrayana. As the three yanas are regarded not just as different levels of the Buddha's teaching but also as successive stages of the path to Supreme Enlightenment, the result is that for Tibetan Buddhism Going for Refuge is simply the means to the arising of the Bodhichitta, and the arising of the Bodhichitta the means to the receiving of abhishekha. In this way the arising of the Bodhichitta comes to be emphasized at the expense of Going for Refuge, even as the receiving of abhishekha comes to be emphasized at the expense of the arising of the Bodhichitta. In other words, Mahayana is emphasized at the expense of Hinayana, Vajrayana at the expense of Mahayana. Although in theory the Buddhism of Tibet is a triyana or 'triple vehicle' Buddhism, in practice it is predominantly tantric in character, and it is as Tantric Buddhism that we usually encounter it in the West.

The fact that the arising of the Bodhichitta is emphasized at the expense of Going for Refuge, and the receiving of abhishekha at the expense of the arising of the Bodhichitta, makes it possible for individual tantric teachings and practices to be emphasized at the expense of the Vajrayana as a whole. Indeed, it makes it possible for them to be emphasized to such an extent that in the end they are taken out of the triyana framework and detached, not from Tibetan Buddhism only but also, like 'vipassana' and 'Zen', from Buddhism itself. This is what has happened in the case of the Dzog-chen or 'Great Perfection' teaching, the ultimate teaching of the Nyingma School, which according to some of its modern exponents has no essential connection with Buddhism. However else we may relate to them, obviously we cannot relate to such people on the basis of a common commitment to the Three Jewels.

Although Tibetan Buddhism regards Going for Refuge to the Buddha, the Dharma, and the Sangha simply as a means to the arising of the Bodhichitta, within the Vajrayana the Three Refuges have an esoteric counterpart known as the Three Roots. These are the Lama or Guru, the root of blessings, the Yidam or Chosen Divinity, the root of accomplishment, and the Dharma Protector, the root of activity. To the extent that the Three Roots represent a recognition, on the part of Tibetan Buddhism, of what may be termed the *principle* of Going for Refuge, as well as a recognition of the fact that at higher levels of spiritual experience this principle may exist in subtler forms, it is to be welcomed. None the less, in Tibetan Buddhism, at least as often encountered in the West, the teaching of the Three Roots can have, in practice, disastrous consequences. It can lead to the perversion of Tibetan Buddhism itself and the betrayal of some of the fundamental principles of the Dharma. To begin with, the importance of the Lama, the root of blessings, is emphasized at the expense of that of the two other roots. The disciple is taught to see the Lama as Buddha and to have unquestioning faith in him. Though such an approach may have a certain validity, when correctly understood, in practice it results, only too often, in the Lama being regarded as infallible (and his behaviour therefore as beyond criticism), as well as in a surrendering, on the part of the disciple, of his (or her) intellectual independence and moral and spiritual autonomy. This is a far cry from the world of the *Kalama-sutta* and from the Buddha's exhortation, as preserved in the Tibetan scriptures themselves, to test his words as the goldsmith tests gold in the fire.

Moreover, the Lama is the *Tantric* Guru. He is the bestower of 'Tantric initiation'. Unfortunately for us in the West, when the Tantras were translated into Tibetan the Sanskrit word *abhishekha*, signifying 'aspersion' or 'sprinkling with water', was rendered as *wangkur* or 'bestowal of power'. This has made possible the adoption of the fashionable term 'empowerment', with all its ideological

connotations, as the standard term for abhishekha or Tantric initiation. Nowadays a lot of people feel deprived of power. But as they want power, and generally want something or someone to 'empower' them, it is not surprising that there should be a widespread demand for *empowerment*, Tantric and otherwise. Where there is a demand, there will be a supply. Tibetan Buddhism in the West would seem to be occupied, to a great extent, with the giving of Tantric initiations. Not only are these initiations advertised in the Buddhist and alternative press; they are open to anyone, Buddhist or non-Buddhist, who is in a position to pay for them, even though according to Vajrayana tradition they are to be given only after one has gone for Refuge and developed the Bodhichitta. Thus there is a wholesale commercialization and vulgarization of Tibetan Buddhism in general and the Vajrayana in particular, a commercialization and vulgarization involving tens of thousands of people and millions of US dollars (it is usually US dollars). There is a lot more I could say on the subject, but I shall leave it for another occasion.

From this very rapid survey it should be evident that while the Theravada, Pure Land Buddhism, Zen, and Tibetan Buddhism, all emphasize what is secondary in Buddhism at the expense of what is primary they do not all emphasize the same secondary thing. The way in which the Order relates to them will therefore vary, at least initially. Yet although they emphasize what is of secondary, even of tertiary, importance in the Buddhist life at the expense of what is primary, each school is based, ultimately, on scriptures and other works in which the centrality of the act of Going for Refuge is made sufficiently clear. It should therefore not be difficult for an open-minded follower of any school to appreciate the importance of that act, at least to an extent, and indeed there are cases where we actually find this happening. In his essay *The Threefold Refuge* the late Nyanaponika Thera explores the meaning of Going for Refuge from the standpoint of a liberal Theravadin, besides trying to find

a way of reviving the practice of Going for Refuge as an act of individual commitment to the Three Jewels, as I and a group of Order members and Mitras discovered when we studied the essay at Padmaloka in the autumn of 1978. Whether any present-day follower of Pure Land Buddhism emphasizes the centrality of Going for Refuge to the Three Jewels I do not know, but I notice that Rennyo, the 'second founder' of the Jōdo Shinshū, in his letters repeatedly refers to the fundamental importance of taking refuge in Amitabha. I also gather, from personal correspondence, that in the Jōdo Shinshū there are two levels of ordination, in both of which the ordinand repeats (apparently in Chinese, with Japanese pronunciation) the standard threefold Refuge-taking formula. In view of the fact that Shakyamuni the historical Buddha and Amitabha the 'archetypal' or even transcendental Buddha are ultimately identical, and the fact that real Going for Refuge and the path of dependence on the 'other power' are in principle synonymous, it should therefore not be difficult for followers of the Jōdo Shinshū to recognize the absolute centrality for the Buddhist life of the act of Going for Refuge.

Followers of Zen should have no difficulty recognizing it either. I have already quoted Tenshin Anderson's moving confession that, astonishing as this might seem, he had never really noticed that he had taken refuge in the Three Jewels and that many Zen students had never even heard about this basic, fundamental practice. How, then, did he come to realize its importance? It was, he tells us, through the teaching and example of Dōgen, the founder (in Japan) of the Sōtō branch of Zen, the branch to which the American abbot himself belongs. Dōgen's last act as he was dying was to circumambulate a pillar on which he had written the words Buddha, Dharma, Sangha, saying as he did so, 'In the beginning, in the middle, and in the end, in your life as you approach death, always, through all births and deaths, always take refuge in Buddha, Dharma, Sangha.'[11] The centrality of the act of Going for Refuge could hardly

be more strikingly affirmed. Tibetan Buddhism can recognize the centrality of Going for Refuge only if it acknowledges that the latter is *not* simply a means to the arising of the Bodhichitta, and we in fact do find at least one eminent contemporary Lama coming close to just such an acknowledgement. In his commentary on the *Samadhiraja Sutra* Thrangu Rinpoche appears to treat 'forming the bodhisattva resolve' and 'taking refuge in the Three Jewels' as *alternative* paths to the development of an extraordinary, as distinct from a mediocre, motivation for Dharma practice.[12]

In our attempts to relate to the Theravada and the Jōdo Shinshū, Zen, and Tibetan Buddhism, we must, therefore, bear in mind that it is possible for each of these schools to come to an appreciation of the importance of Going for Refuge in the light of its own tradition. This brings me to my third and last principle, with which I shall be dealing more briefly than I have dealt with the principle of ecumenicity and the principle of orthodoxy.

The Principle of Personal Contact

In some of my writings and lectures I have spoken in terms of the group and the individual, and distinguished the individual (who is not the individual*ist*) from what I call the 'group member'. One who goes effectively for Refuge is *ipso facto* an individual. Indeed only an individual *can* go for Refuge in this way, though a group member is of course capable of an ethnic or cultural Going for Refuge, which strictly speaking is not a Going for Refuge at all. Order members, by virtue of their (at least) effective Going for Refuge are individuals, and their 'membership' of the Order is therefore not a group membership. It is not a group membership because the Order itself is not a group but something for which we have no word in the English language but which may be termed a spiritual community, in the sense of a community united by what its 'members' have in common *spiritually*, that is, by their common

commitment to the Three Jewels. When I speak of the relation of the Order to the rest of the Buddhist world, which in practice means its relation to the Theravada, to Pure Land Buddhism, to Zen, and to Tibetan Buddhism, I am therefore not speaking of the relation of one 'Buddhist group' to other 'Buddhist groups'. In the words with which I ended my paper on the History of My Going for Refuge, and which I have already quoted at the beginning of this paper, the relation of the Order to the rest of the Buddhist world is a relation that subsists, essentially, with individuals.

This is not to say that the Order does not have relations, through the FWBO Communications Office and in other ways, with a number of different Buddhist organizations, even though these organizations do think of themselves as being 'Buddhist groups' and of the FWBO (the Order included) as being likewise a Buddhist group. The FWBO is in fact an active member of the European Buddhist Union, as well as being a member, through the Poona TBMSG, of the World Fellowship of Buddhists. In relating to these bodies, however, we attach the greatest importance to personal contact. Those of us who have the responsibility of liaising with 'other' Buddhist groups therefore do our best to relate to them in our capacity *as individuals*, not just as faceless 'representatives' of the FWBO. It is as individuals – individuals who have gone for Refuge to the Three Jewels – that we extend to them the hand of spiritual fellowship, in this way seeking to place the relationship between the Order and their organization on the basis of friendship between some at least of our respective members. Only on such a basis, I believe, is genuine co-operation between different parts of the Buddhist world really possible. None the less, we have not found it easy to develop the kind of friendship to which I have referred. Buddhist organizations, accustomed as they generally are to thinking of their relations with other Buddhist groups in collective, 'political' terms, find it difficult to grasp the idea of placing those relations on the basis of personal friendship between individuals or even to

understand what the Order is getting at when it talks in this way. There is also the fact that in many parts of the Western world the ideal and institution of friendship, especially friendship between men, has lost much of its traditional significance and is even regarded with suspicion. All the same, we continue to extend the hand of spiritual fellowship to the representatives of such Buddhist groups as we are in contact with, in the hope they will reciprocate, as some of them have indeed already started doing.

In extending that hand there are a number of considerations that we have to bear in mind, both in justice to ourselves and out of respect for others. Subhuti has dealt with most of them in the third part of the lecture to which I have already referred, and there is no need for me to go over the same ground. In any case, I have promised to deal with the principle of personal contact more briefly than I have dealt with the two other principles. I shall therefore confine myself to making three points, which could perhaps be known as Three Points for Order Members Relating to the Rest of the Buddhist World, which in practice of course means Order members relating to individual followers of the Theravada, Pure Land Buddhism, Zen, and Tibetan Buddhism. Before I make these points, however, I would like to emphasize a point of a much more general nature, the importance of which should not be overlooked. As you know, in the Order we practise – and teach – the metta-bhavana or 'development of loving-kindness' meditation, in which feelings of ardent goodwill are successively directed to oneself, a friend, a neutral person, an enemy, and, eventually, to all living beings. But this does not mean that metta is something one experiences only when seated on the meditation cushion. Far from it. Metta or loving-kindness is an emotion which ideally the Buddhist should feel at all times (at least when awake), in all places, and with regard to every person – and every animal – with whom he (or she) comes in contact, irrespective of that person's nationality, race, religion, age, social position, or sexual orientation. Extending the

hand of spiritual fellowship to other Buddhists thus does not exclude the possibility of friendship with those who are not Buddhists. In principle we extend the hand of friendship to all. Our deepest friendships, however, at least potentially, will always be with those who, like us, go for Refuge to the Three Jewels, especially when for them, too, the act of Going for Refuge is the central act of the Buddhist life. The important point of a more general nature having been made, now for my Three Points for Order Members Relating to the Rest of the Buddhist World.

First point: Do not allow yourself to be put in a false position. According to the dictionary, a false position is 'a situation in which a person is forced to act or seems to be acting against his principles or interests' (*Collins*), or, more succinctly, 'one in which [a] person must seem to act against his principles' (*Concise Oxford*). An Order member is in a false position when he (or she) appears to behave as though he was not an Order member, that is, appears to behave as though he was not one who (at least) effectively goes for Refuge to the Three Jewels and for whom Going for Refuge is the central, definitive act of the Buddhist life. In other words, an Order member is in a false position when he (or she) appears to behave as though he was not, in fact, a real Buddhist and not one for whom, moreover, commitment is primary, lifestyle secondary. A simple and obvious example of the way in which an Order member may be put in this position is what happens when he meets a Theravadin bhikkhu. The Theravada, of course, sees the Buddhist community as being divided into two distinct groups, that of the monks, who alone are the real Buddhists, and that of the laity, who are the not-so-real Buddhists. As the Order Member does not wear a yellow robe, and is not shaven-headed, the bhikkhu will therefore assume that, if he is a Buddhist at all, he is a lay Buddhist, and will treat him accordingly, as I have already pointed out when dealing with the principle of orthodoxy. He may, in all innocence, even ask the Order member how many times a year he visits the local (Theravadin) temple and

makes offerings to the monks. This is like being asked whether one has stopped beating one's mother. The Order member will be able to 'answer' the bhikkhu's question only by challenging his assumptions, which will necessarily involve going into such matters as the difference between commitment and lifestyle and the importance of *not* emphasizing the latter at the expense of the former. All this may well take time, especially if the bhikkhu finds it difficult to understand what the Order member is getting at, and in any case the Order member will be able to challenge the bhikkhu only if he is firmly established in his own Going for Refuge and has a thorough grasp of the principles on which the Order is based. But whether or not it takes time, and whether or not the bhikkhu has difficulty understanding what he is getting at, the Order member will conduct his side of the discussion with courtesy, tact, and good humour.

There are a number of other ways in which an Order member may be put in a false position, and appear not to be a real Buddhist. He (or she) may be asked if he practises 'insight meditation', the assumption being, in this case, that if one is not practising vipassana in its modern 'Burmese' form one is not really meditating at all and has no spiritual life worth mentioning. Similarly, an Order member may be asked how many Zen sesshins he has attended or which Tantric initiations he has received from which Tibetan lamas. In these cases, too, he will 'answer' the question by challenging the assumptions on which it is based in the way I have indicated.

Second Point: Look for the deepest common ground. Here the emphasis is on 'deepest'. Human beings have a lot of things in common. To begin with, they have in common the fact that they are members of the human race – that they are all risen apes or fallen angels or both. It is because human beings are basically one that it is possible, as I once told a Bombay audience I truly and deeply believed, for us to communicate with any other human being, to feel for any other human being, to be friends with any other human

being. But there are levels of communication; there are levels of friendship. Ideally, an Order member should relate to the representative of a Buddhist group on the basis of what they have in common *as Buddhists*, rather than on the basis of a common interest in, for example, vintage motor cars or triangular postage stamps or on the basis of the fact that both parties happen to be parents or attended the same public school – though all these can, of course, serve as points of departure. What Buddhists have in common, as Buddhists, is the fact that they all go for Refuge to the Three Jewels. There are, however, a number of different levels of Going for Refuge: ethnic (or cultural), provisional, effective, real, and absolute. In relating to other Buddhists the Order member should try, initially, to ascertain the level of their Going for Refuge. In particular, he (or she) should try to ascertain whether it is ethnic or effective, all the time being open to the possibility that it is real. If their Going for Refuge is merely ethnic, or has a strong ethnic or cultural tinge, then it will be difficult, even impossible, to communicate and be friends with them as though they were true Buddhists. At best you and they will be able to relate as members of your respective 'Buddhist groups', whether larger or smaller, which means relating collectively and 'politically' rather than individually and spiritually. Should the Going for Refuge of the other Buddhists be effective, however, then between them and the Order member there will exist genuine common ground, and this common ground will be all the deeper if the other Buddhists are able to recognize not only that Going for Refuge is what all Buddhists have in common but also that it is the most important thing they have in common and central to the Buddhist life. One way an Order member can help other Buddhists recognize the importance and centrality of the act of Going for Refuge is by drawing their attention to passages in their own scriptures where this is made clear. Naturally, the Order member will be able to do this only if he (or she) has a good knowledge of those scriptures and is familiar, moreover, with

the principal tenets of the school or schools to which the other Buddhists happen to belong.

Third Point: Do not be misled by labels. In ordinary life labels are useful, even indispensable. But they can also be misleading, especially where human beings are concerned. Within the field of Buddhism the terms Mahayanist and Hinayanist are a case in point. A Mahayanist or follower of the Great Way is not always dedicated to the salvation of all sentient beings, nor is a Hinayanist invariably preoccupied with his own emancipation from suffering. 'Mahayanists' may in actual fact be mean and selfish, 'Hinayanists' warm-hearted and generous. For this reason it has been suggested that the terms Hinayana and Mahayana should be understood as referring not so much to schools and doctrines as to spiritual attitudes and orientations. Labels often take the form of styles and titles. In recent years the Buddhist world has witnessed the appearance on the scene of a perfect swarm of 'His Holinesses' and 'His Eminences', not all of them necessarily either holy or spiritually eminent. Originally, it seems, only the Dalai Lama was accorded the style of 'His Holiness' in international diplomatic usage, on the grounds that like the Pope he was both head of state and head of religion. The Panchen Lama was styled 'His Eminence', presumably because his position was analogous to that of a cardinal. In 1956, when the Indian government invited the two Grand Lamas to visit India, the Chinese insisted, as a condition of their allowing the visit to take place, that the same protocol should be observed for both and the Panchen Lama, too, be accorded the style of 'His Holiness'. The motive for this insistence on the part of the Chinese was, of course, purely political. Subsequently, the Karmapa started styling himself 'His Holiness', with the result that such self-promotion soon became widespread, with more and more Buddhist teachers – not all of them Tibetan – calling themselves either 'His Holiness' or 'His Eminence'. Labels can also take the form of more traditional styles and titles such as 'Sangharaja' and 'Nayaka Maha Thera', and these

too can be misleading; nor must we forget that not everyone styling himself a 'meditation teacher' meditates and that a 'forest monk' may not actually live in the forest. Whatever the label may be, in relating to other Buddhists an Order member should do his (or her) best to relate not to the label but to the person behind the label, to relate on the basis of the Going for Refuge common to all Buddhists, and to relate on the deepest possible level of that Going for Refuge. Not that labels can be ignored completely, even if only because other people take them seriously; but if they cannot be ignored, they should at least not be allowed to mislead.

So much, then, for my Three Points. So much for the relation of the Order to the rest of the Buddhist world. Though issues already dealt with elsewhere have not been touched on, in this paper I have covered a good deal of ground. We saw that since I spoke on the History of My Going for Refuge, eight years ago, the Order has grown not only numerically but in 'collective' maturity and experience, while the FWBO's activities have expanded and diversified. I have therefore been able to hand on many of my responsibilities as founder and head of the Order, and hope soon to have handed them all on. In connection with what I called the Principle of Ecumenicity we saw that instead of one Buddhist world there are a number of sectarian Buddhist worlds, and that for all practical purposes the Order has separate relations with the Theravada, the Jōdo Shinshū, Zen, and Tibetan Buddhism. Each of these schools has its own general characteristics and its own scriptures, from all of which we in the Order derive inspiration and guidance. We also saw, in connection with this principle, that during the last fifty years the portion of the earth's surface traditionally covered by Buddhism has shrunk dramatically, so that despite important accessions in India and the West Buddhism was now the smallest and in certain respects the least influential of the three great world religions. The Principle of Orthodoxy enabled me, incidentally, to connect my earlier with my later teaching. An orthodox Buddhist,

we saw, was one for whom Going for Refuge was primary, observance of the precepts (and practice of meditation etc.) secondary, and lifestyle tertiary. The Theravada was not orthodox because of its emphasis on monasticism, the Jōdo Shinshū because of its emphasis on the laical lifestyle, Zen because of its emphasis on meditation, and Tibetan Buddhism because of its emphasis on Tantric initiation. None the less, as we also saw, all these schools were based on scriptures and other works in which the centrality of the act of Going for Refuge is made sufficiently clear. In connection with the Principle of Personal Contact we saw that those of us who have the responsibility for liaising with 'other' Buddhist groups do so in our capacity as individuals, and that while our deepest friendships may be with those who, like us, go for Refuge to the Three Jewels, in principle we extend the hand of fellowship to all. I also had Three Points for Order Members Relating to the Rest of the Buddhist World: Do not allow yourself to be put in a false position; Look for the deepest common ground; and, Do not be misled by labels. These points having been made, I have now finished sharing with you my current thinking about the relation of the Order to the rest of the Buddhist world. The promise of eight years ago has been redeemed.

References

1 Sangharakshita, *A Survey of Buddhism*, 7th edition, Windhorse 1993, p.325 *et seq.*
2 *Tricycle: The Buddhist Review Vol.V*, no.2 (Winter 1995), p.53
3 Simon Midgeley and Philip Sherwell, *The Daily Telegraph*, Monday 15 January 1996, pp.1–2
4 Keith Dowman, 'Himalayan Intrigue: The Search for the new Karmapa', *Tricycle: The Buddhist Review vol.II*, no.2 (Winter 1992), pp.29–34
5 Reginald A. Ray, *Buddhist Saints in India: A Study in Buddhist Values and Orientations*, Oxford University Press 1994, p.62
6 Urgyen Sangharakshita, review of *Buddhist Saints in India*, in *The Times Higher Education Supplement*, 17 February 1995
7 I.B. Horner, *The Middle Way*, vol.32, no.1 (May 1957), p.13
8 Sangharakshita, *The Meaning of Orthodoxy in Buddhism: A Protest*, Windhorse Publications, Glasgow, pp.15–21
9 Abbot Tenshin Anderson, 'Speaking the Unspoken' Talk One, *Shambhala Sun*, (June 1993), p.31
10 *Life with a Capital 'L'*. An interview with Philip Kapleau Roshi. *Tricycle*: The Buddhist Review, (Summer 1993), pp.55–56

11 Abbot Tenshin Anderson, 'Speaking the Unspoken' Talk One, *Shambhala Sun* (June 1993), p.31

12 Thrangu Rinpoche, *King of Samadhi: Commentaries on The Samadhi Raja Sutra & The Song of Lodro Thaye*, Rangjung Yeshe Publications, Hong Kong, Boudhnath & Arhus, 1994, p.39

The Windhorse symbolizes the energy of the enlightened mind carrying the Three Jewels – the Buddha, the Dharma, and the Sangha – to all sentient beings.

Buddhism is one of the fastest growing spiritual traditions in the Western world. Throughout its 2,500-year history, it has always succeeded in adapting its mode of expression to suit whatever culture it has encountered.

Windhorse Publications aims to continue this tradition as Buddhism comes to the West. Today's Westerners are heirs to the entire Buddhist tradition, free to draw instruction and inspiration from all the many schools and branches. Windhorse publishes works by authors who not only understand the Buddhist tradition but are also familiar with Western culture and the Western mind.

For orders and catalogues contact:

WINDHORSE PUBLICATIONS

UNIT 1-316

THE CUSTARD FACTORY

GIBB STREET

BIRMINGHAM   B9 4AA

UK

WINDHORSE PUBLICATIONS INC

14 HEARTWOOD CIRCLE

NEWMARKET

NEW HAMPSHIRE 03857

USA

Windhorse Publications is an arm of the Friends of the Western Buddhist Order, which has more than sixty centres on four continents. Through these centres, members of the Western Buddhist Order offer regular programmes of events for the general public and for more experienced students. These include meditation classes, public talks, study on Buddhist themes and texts, and 'bodywork' classes such as t'ai chi, yoga, and massage. The FWBO also runs several retreat centres and the Karuna Trust, a fundraising charity that supports social welfare projects in the slums and villages of India.

Many FWBO centres have residential spiritual communities and ethical businesses associated with them. Arts activities are encouraged too, as is the development of strong bonds of friendship between people who share the same ideals. In this way the FWBO is developing a unique approach to Buddhism, not simply as a set of techniques, less still as an exotic cultural interest, but as a creatively directed way of life for people living in the modern world.

If you would like more information about the FWBO please write to:

LONDON BUDDHIST CENTRE	ARYALOKA
51 ROMAN ROAD	14 HEARTWOOD CIRCLE
LONDON	NEWMARKET
E2 0HU	NEW HAMPSHIRE 03857
UK	USA

Also From Windhorse

SANGHARAKSHITA
THE HISTORY OF MY GOING FOR REFUGE

The founder of the Western Buddhist Order traces the 'erratic process of discovery' that has led him to conclude that the monastic life-style and spiritual life are not identical, that it is possible to be a good monk or nun and at the same time a bad Buddhist, and that Going for Refuge – the act of commitment to Buddhist spiritual ideals – is the central and definitive act of the Buddhist life, and the fundamental basis of unity among Buddhists.

For anyone concerned with the spiritual vitality of the Buddhist tradition – and with its transmission in the modern world – this meticulously plotted 'history' makes indispensable reading.

130 pages
£4.95/$9.95
ISBN 0 904766 33 0

SANGHARAKSHITA
MY RELATION TO THE ORDER

In this heartfelt communication, Sangharakshita reflects on his personal involvement with the Western Buddhist Order, the spiritual community which he established in 1968. As founder, teacher, and initial preceptor, Sangharakshita has seen the Order spread throughout the world and has nurtured its development as an effective force for the introduction of Buddhism to the modern world.

Speaking on the twenty-second anniversary of the Order's founding, his voice is above all that of a friend, alive with warmth, wit, and candour.

Of particular interest to many will be Sangharakshita's comments on the continually evolving 'process' through which the Order encourages and helps people to go for Refuge and thus join its ranks.

36 pages
ISBN 0 904766 47 0
£1.95/$3.95

SUBHUTI

BRINGING BUDDHISM TO THE WEST: A LIFE OF SANGHARAKSHITA

Born in London, Dennis Lingwood realized that he was a Buddhist at the age of sixteen. Conscripted during the Second World War, army life took him to India where he stayed on to become the Buddhist monk, Sangharakshita. By the mid-fifties he was an increasingly active and forthright exponent of Buddhism, and had established a uniquely non-sectarian centre in Kalimpong.

As hippies flocked eastward in the sixties, Sangharakshita returned to England to establish the Friends of the Western Buddhist Order. This movement has been pioneering a vital form of Buddhism for the modern world. It is also at the heart of a Buddhist revival in India – the land where Buddhism was born 2,500 years ago.

Sangharakshita's story is proof that it is possible to live a truly spiritual life in the modern world.

208 pages, with photographs
ISBN 0 904766 69 1
£9.99/$18.95

SUBHUTI

SANGHARAKSHITA: A NEW VOICE IN THE BUDDHIST TRADITION

Sangharakshita was one of the first Westerners to make the journey to the East and to don the monk's yellow robe. In India he gained unique experience in the main traditions of Buddhist teaching and practice. His involvement with the 'mass conversion' of ex-Untouchable Hindus to Buddhism exposed him to a revolutionary new experiment in social transformation. More recently he founded one of the most successful Buddhist movements in the modern world – pioneering a 'living Buddhism' that seems ideally suited to our times.

Highly respected as an outspoken writer and commentator, he has never been afraid to communicate his insights and views, even if they challenge venerated elements of Buddhist tradition.

But what are those insights and views? How have they arisen and developed? Here one of Sangharakshita's leading disciples offers an account of his evolution as a thinker ~~and~~ ~~~~ ~~~~.

328 pagr~
ISBN 0
£9.99, $